FREEHAND DRAWING
for Architects and Designers

FREEHAND DRAWING

for Architects and Designers

WATERCOLOR
COLORED PENCIL
BLACK AND WHITE TECHNIQUES

Erwin Herzberger

Whitney Library of Design

An imprint of Watson-Guptill Publications/New York

Copyright © 1988 Karl Krämer Verlag Stuttgart

First published in the United States in 1996 by Whitney Library of Design,
an imprint of Watson-Guptill Publications, a division of BPI Communications, Inc.,
1515 Broadway, New York, NY 10036.

Library of Congress Cataloging-in-Publication Data

Herzberger, Erwin.
  [Freihandzeichnen, English]
  Freehand drawing for architects and designers: watercolor, colored
  pencil, and black and white techniques / Erwin Herzberger.
    p. cm.
  Includes index.
  ISBN 0-8230-1919-5
  1. Architectural drawing—Technique. I. Title.
  NA2708.H4713 1996   95-50296
  720'.28'4--dc20   CIP

Front and back cover design: Abigail Sturges

Manufactured in Italy

First printing, 1996

1 2 3 4 5 6 7 8 9 / 02 01 00 99 98 97 96

Introduction

The aim of this book is to create an awareness of the two main criteria essential to the development of drawing skills: technique and logic.

A person inexperienced in drawing will initially try to acquire certain techniques. The experienced draughtsman is more likely to be interested in the perfection of technical abilities and methods. For these reasons the didactic steps begin with simple, basic considerations. The more complex, systematic information is built up on this. Although it is necessary to cite models, the student of drawing should always attempt to overcome the inevitable (and necessary) initial tendency merely to copy, and should try to find a drawing language of his or her own. Nothing is more fatal than the slavish imitation of a particular style of drawing; for one's own graphic and mental development will be limited, if not impeded, by this. The book is therefore not meant to represent a »school of drawing« in the usual sense of that term. Nor are the basic technical graphic skills presented in the form of formulae; (e.g. how to draw a horse or a dog). All objects are forms in space. Bearing this in mind, the reader should be helped to reach a point where, depending on the technical information available, he or she will be able to develop a drawing systematically and independently, and to experiment and practise personal graphic skills in a free and easy manner. The fact that many illustrations take the form of actual studies in drawing is meant to enable the learner to make comparisons between the different ways in which a drawing can be created. It should also help eliminate inhibitions caused by the fear of making mistakes in one's own drawings.

In accordance with this didactic concept, the book begins with line drawings, followed by an explanation of the use of guide or construction lines, enveloping volumes and perspective. After these basic systematic considerations, various methods of hatching are discussed, from which it is but a short step to coloured pencil and crayon work. The book ends with an examination of water-colour technique, as a further development of drawing skills. This section begins with drawings to which water-colours are applied subsequently and goes on to consider the gradual reduction of the preliminary drawing (with increasing emphasis on coloration), concluding with freely painted studies in which the drawn element is scarcely of any significance any more.

This graduated system, in which technical information and the relationship between various methods are communicated step by step, makes independent learning a challenge, and at the same time allows the reader the opportunity to develop his or her own graphic personality.

Contents

ANALYTICAL DRAWING

COLOURED PENCIL TECHNIQUE

WATER-COLOUR TECHNIQUE

Implements and Materials

The nature of any depiction is influenced by the choice of drawing implements and materials. There is little point, therefore, in recommending one
particular medium or material rather than another, especially as the various
grounds on which one draws – e.g. paper or card – have different properties
and thus exert a further influence on the appearance of a drawing.

For the beginner this means that he should not merely exercise the art of
drawing, but should also experiment with different implements and with different types of paper. Instead of providing a list of every conceivable combination, mention will be made of the special characteristics that should be
taken into account, when selecting materials.

Characteristics of Drawing Implements

One can differentiate fundamentally between drawing techniques based on
a process of abrasion or rubbing (e.g. pencil, charcoal, crayon) and those in
which fluids (e.g. Indian or other inks) are applied by means of a pen or the
like. In the former case the lines drawn will be influenced by the degree of
hardness of the pencil, lead, etc. used. In the latter case it is the elasticity or
the thickness of the nib that determines the character of the line. In physical
terms it is the interaction of the forces brought into play – the weight of the
drawing implement, the firmness of hand with which one draws, the force
of friction between implement and the surface drawn upon – that should be
felt and in which one should gain experience in drawing exercises. The
length of the drawing implement used and the position of its centre of gravity play a crucial role in this respect. Implements that are too long or too short
can have a negative effect on a drawing.

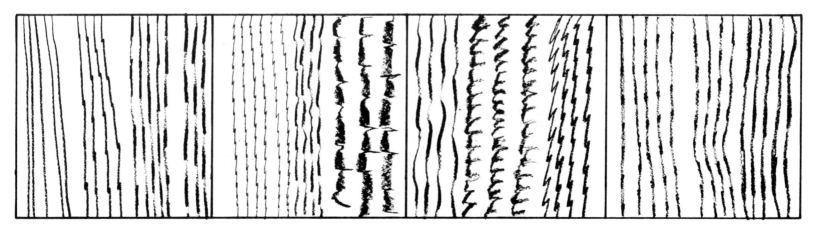

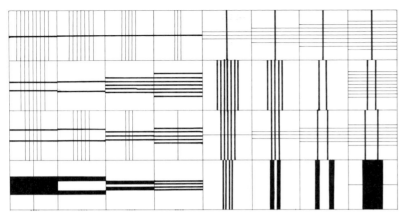

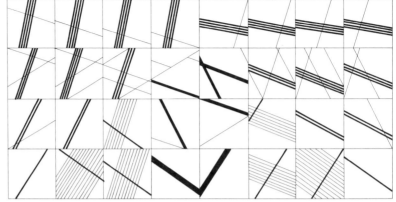

Comparison between lines drawn with a straight-edge (above) and free-hand lines (below).

Properties of Drawing Surface

Paper, art board, etc. can be soft or hard, rough or smooth in texture. Depending on the combination of implement and paper used, a variety of individual graphic effects can be achieved. Only by an extensive process of trial and error can one assess the broad range of qualities different papers possess. The draughtsman himself should co-ordinate the combination of implement and working surface to the expression he wishes to achieve in his drawing. Transparent drawing paper, for example, is relatively rough, and even with 4H or 6H leads sufficient friction will be created to achieve a clear line. In the case of soft papers, however, (e.g. newspaper) this degree of pencil hardness produces very weak lines. Using a ball-point pen to draw on rough-textured paper will produce a broken line; whereas on smooth, soft paper, such as offset paper, the line will be a fine homogeneous one.

The list of combinations of this kind could be extended at will. An awareness of them and the effects to be achieved with them belongs to the foundations of technical skill. The type of line one draws – homogeneous, fluctuating or broken – is influenced by these criteria. Experienced draughtsmen will lay a ground on their paper using their own particular method, one form being a coloured ground. Nowadays specialist dealers offer high-quality drawing card (which is admittedly not cheap) in a range of different sizings, surface textures and weights.

If one wishes to draw on or, more especially, apply a wash to water-colour paper or cartridge paper, one should also be aware of the absorption quality of the paper and the degree to which it will stretch or warp when wetted, as well as the abrasive quality of the surface after repeated working.

Application of colour with brush, using diluted drawing ink. By using a frottage or rubbing technique, textures can be obtained that are made up of areas of very fine dots or lines.

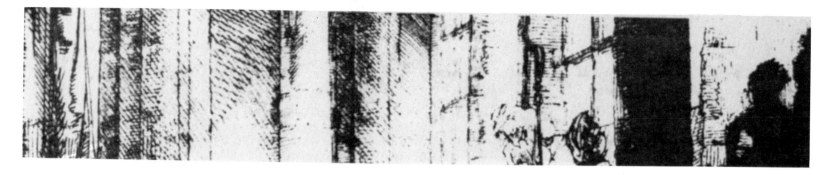

Light-dark tones created by overlaying
free-hand shading. Section from a
drawing from Rembrandt.

Light-dark range of tones: pencil on 130 g
drawing paper with slightly rough
surface; hardness of leads 2H-6B.

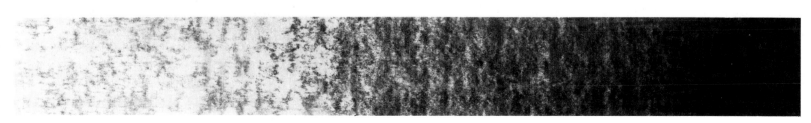

Charcoal on water-colour paper.

1.) Der Mond ist aufgegangen, die güldnen
Sternlein prangen am Himmel hell und
klar. Der Wald steht schwarz und schwei-
get und ausden Wiesen steiget der weiße
Nebel wunderbar.   /14

and oh my love for you has no more room to
grow, Ginny come lately, my dream come
true. You may have come lately, but Ginny
come lately. I'm in love with you.-

Ten thousand people may be more
People talking without speaking
People hearing without listening
People writing songs that voices...

, your letters they all say that you're beside
me now / then why do I feel alone ?
I'm standing on a ledge and your fine
spider web / Is fastening my ankle to
symmetrien, geometrische ordnungen,
rhythmische folgen sein, aber auch
und schatten, Plastizität und Far-
keit können zur Thematisierung d
bildes beitragen. Wirklich ist es die
tung des Objekts an seinem Ort, die den
[illegible] [illegible] [illegible] mit ihm,

Hand and Body Movements

Just as everyone develops his own personal style of handwriting, so too, with the appropriate training, everyone can acquire his own individual style of drawing. Some ›schools of drawing‹ inhibit the development of personal characteristics more than they stimulate them. For that reason the reader is strongly advised not to try to adopt a particular style. Everyone should develop his own manner of drawing in accordance with his abilities.

The interacting motions of fingers, hand, and arm and even the body – in the case of larger-scale works – all have an influence on the way one draws. The work of a beginner, which as a rule will be drawn with a more hesitant stroke, will differ strikingly from that produced by the fluent technique of a »professional«. But in many cases the fluently drawn work will be overrated purely for its graphic sophistication, – a problem that will be examined in detail later. As everyone knows, a person's handwriting undergoes numerous transformations from childhood onwards. In the same way the manner and facility of drawing are subject to change.

Beginners often work to a small scale (A4 or A5) and draw merely with their fingertips, without using the hand and forearm. The normal range of bodily gestures is not employed, and as a consequence most drawings are made with short strokes (and often using hard leads). The end product is remarkably expressionless. With larger-scale works (A2 and upwards) one cannot avoid bringing the arm, indeed the whole body, into play in the drawing process. As a result of this, a much greater differentiation of line is achieved; and one has considerably more control in drawing thin light lines or indeed thick heavy ones. Drawings acquire their individual expression through the movements of the body.

Scale, implements and background material should therefore be used in a more conscious manner. With pencils or drawing pens variable lines can be achieved simply by changing the pressure. The use of felt-tip pens or instruments with a tube-like nib, on the other hand, leads to a more homogeneous and sometimes sterile line character. In order to broaden one's experience, it is very important to ring the changes with the implements and materials one uses and to vary the scale to which one works.

STADTKIRCHE IN SCHORNDORF.

Handwriting at the ages of 14, 17, 20, 25 and 35.

Two drawings by the same person: at the age of 17 (top), and 35 (bottom).

13

Bodily motion, together with the control of the whole apparatus of movement, is very strongly dependent on a person's psychological attitude. Shyness at creating a clumsy drawing is influenced by the psyche; at the same time, it also has a great influence on our bodily movement as a whole. The lack of inhibition children usually show when painting is missing in many people in later years. In addition there is often a desire to create a »beautiful« drawing, in the process of which a free, searching manner of sketching is suppressed. Furthermore, if a person feels he is being watched, the desire for success will become compulsive – at least where a person has not learnt to overcome this inhibition. The ability to sit down amongst other people in a relaxed manner and, without any great show, to draw with pleasure without feeling oneself observed is certainly something many people have to train. Only with a relaxed attitude free of anxiety is it possible to experiment in drawing.

The drawings of a 7 and 5-year-old child. The adult objection that one creature is all head and feet and has no body overlooks the representational context of a child when drawing.

Free-hand studies. Acceptance of errors
in a drawing; repeated attempts.

Steps in Drawing

Before proceeding to deal with the basic technical skills and graphical aspects of drawing, one possible misapprehension should be ruled out at this point: that is the assumption that drawing can only be learned in the manner described here. In this respect one could compare drawing with dancing, where the training a person receives is based on learning a number of fundamental steps. These, when linked together, enable a dance to be created. On the other hand, one must ask whether it is not dancing, when a person without any such training ventures a few unconventional steps. Everyone should be encouraged to follow the path that suits his own particular inclinations best, whether it be a formal academic one or his own intuition.

Finger Exercises

So-called »finger exercises« help to extend a person's experience of the various characteristics of materials and implements; they also provide concrete basic practice in line drawing and the creation of graphic structures. The purpose of such exercises is limited, but it is useful to be acquainted with the basic criteria of graphics.

Straight free-hand lines will usually exhibit a series of deviations up and down. By keeping these as small as possible, the overall impression will be that of a straight line.

Curved and circular lines should be drawn as precisely as possible; freely curving lines, in accordance with a regular or random pattern.

Examples of simple finger exercises:
graphic patterns. (The illustrations have
been reduced to roughly half their original
size.)

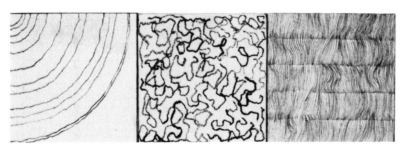
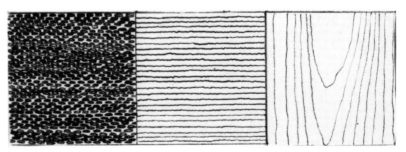

Use of simple graphic patterns to create
a free, planar composition.

Corrections During the Drawing Process

Correcting mistakes is, psychologically speaking, a very important process. If a person corrects errors instead of erasing them, he is admitting them to himself and to others. Furthermore, the creative process behind a sketch and above all its quality remain visible subsequently, and one can trace the stages in its realization. A person who does not erase the mistakes in his sketches can quickly see how he should obviate them. That is why it is sensible to repeat sketches as often as necessary, rather than to feign flawlessness by means of a laborious process of retouching.

It is also advisible not to inscribe the outline of an object indelibly on the paper by means of a thick black line, but to suggest the relative positions and dimensions of the whole and its parts by means of fine lines, (not using a hard lead). The eye will then be able to seek the right line amidst the overall network of lines, and, by a gradual process of intensification, the object will come to assume form — both in outline and in its surface quality. A completely worked out graphical study has little purpose at this stage of drawing.

Lines drawn in the wrong position are corrected by drawing over them repeatedly.

Joseph Maria Olbrich: Station building
for the Stadtbahn in Vienna. Perspective
sketch. Drawing ink.

The Draft Sketch

Close observation is a prerequisite of drawing. The draughtsman has to recognize and depict vertical, horizontal, oblique, curved and irregular lines. In order to be able to draw an object, it is necessary first of all to identify its formal characteristics. In the course of the drawing process one develops an increasing consciousness on an intellectual plane. If these two abilities are not trained and developed, the draughtsman's skills will not rise above the level of mere reproduction.

With the exception of basic geometric volumes, all objects are articulated to a greater or lesser extent into various components, and a hierarchy within the volumetric divisions can usually be established. One differentiates between overall, large-scale form, small-scale form and details. The borders between these are fluid and should be determined in each case on the basis of the object to be depicted. In the case of objects of a geometric composition (e.g. architecture) the division into these three categories is usually obvious. With objects found in nature, however, this subdivision can be difficult, since the forms encountered are frequently irregular, curved or winding, intertwining, etc. At all events it is the task of the draughtsman to differentiate mentally between overall forms and smaller components on the basis of logical consideration, and to translate these on to paper as part of the drawing process.

It would seem logical to begin by sketching the major elements, omitting detailed expression at the outset. Anyone to whom this form of perception is alien, should imagine the object he wishes to draw covered by white paper or cloth. The smaller-scale forms and details would then be covered up and only the overall form identifiable. The translation of this intellectual process into drawing gives rise to a draft or preliminary sketch, in which only the main components and their overall relationship and articulation are represented.

In addition to the didactic element of learning to see in this way, this approach also has a practical advantage. The possible errors one could make in drawing the object are reduced in number, if all one has to do is enter the subsidiary forms and details in the draft sketch. With the opposite approach – i.e. starting off by drawing the details – there is a danger that errors of draughtsmanship will accumulate as one adds more and more small-scale components, resulting in a distortion of the overall form. Furthermore, it is clear that, quite apart from the technical aspect of drawing, the intellectual process involved is illogical.

The sketches of a wine glass and a chair serve to illustrate this. Objects should initially be drawn orthogonally and then from an oblique angle.

The basic form of a covered object is clearly visible.

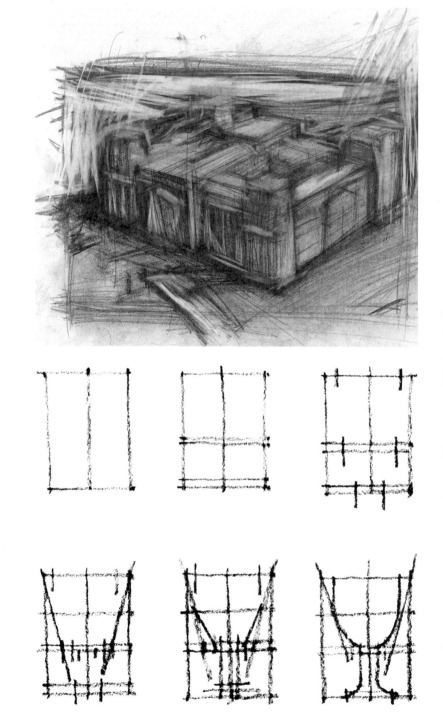

System of constructing a draft sketch of an object, using a glass as an example
1. Outer envelope enclosing the entire object
2. Central axis and horizontal articulation
3. Vertical articulation
4. Diagonal guide lines
5. Further refinement and details
6. Contours drawn in

By drawing simple, straight lines it is possible to define the volumetric outline and indeed the edges of the object itself by means of plane surfaces. Gradually a network of lines is built up within the overall form of the object. Where drawing errors occur, these should be corrected *without* erasing the wrongly drawn lines: otherwise all possibility of recapitulating the process of development the work has undergone will be removed.

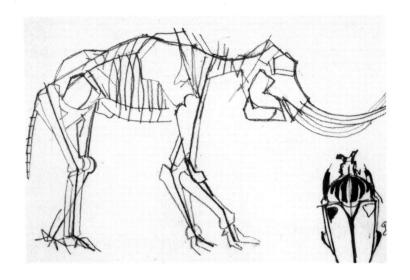

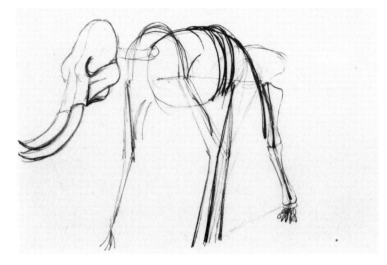

Draft sketches of a skeleton (Steinheim mammoth). In the repeated drawing of lines one can follow the initial search for the actual position of body, skull and limbs. In further stages of the work smaller-scale forms (e.g. thigh bone and tibia) and details (ribs, tarsal bone) are elaborated.

The architectural object is reduced to its overall form (the hull of the building) and the main smaller-scale forms (oriel windows, central tower, steps). The shapes of the caps to the towers are simplified. There would be no problem in correcting drawing errors relating to proportions at this stage. Surface details are entered in the draft sketch: in this case, windows, shutters, timber framing, masonry, etc.

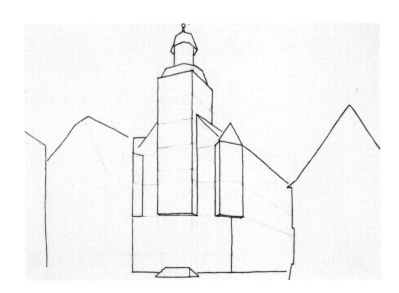

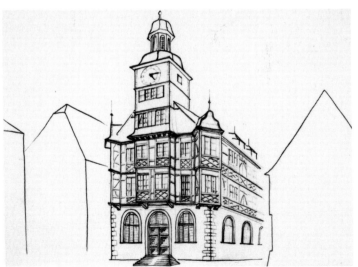

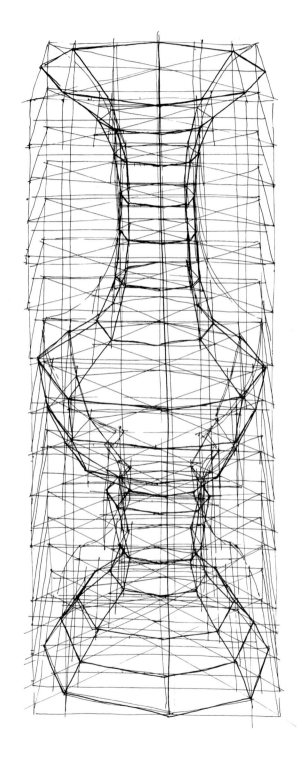

Guide Lines and Enveloping Volumes

All lines that help to determine the form of an object by means of approximation are referred to as guide or construction lines. Enveloping volumes are imaginary volumes representing the approximate enclosing form of an object. Both these terms are related in systematic drawing technique, the basic quality of which lies in the rational method with which these drawing aids are applied. As the illustrations show, not merely simple forms, but complex, twisted shapes can be defined with the help of straight or angled construction lines. The form to be drawn is reduced to a series of small-scale geometric planes adjoining each other. In further stages of the work the object can be drawn in over this planar or spatial framework with a bolder line.

In order to approach the object in a systematic way, it should be drawn initially without perspective foreshortening, in order to acquaint oneself with the relative proportions, (cf. p. 21). Having familiarized oneself with these aspects, one should now attempt to develop the frontal articulation into a sculptural, three-dimensional form. In the case of a simple object, such as a glass, no great problems are involved in this. But it is much more difficult to bring out the sculptural form of a volume of complicated shape, such as a human head. By means of careful observation, one should determine which surface planes can be linked together and simplified and what line will best describe the actual form of the object. The ›rational approach‹ mentioned at the beginning is here decisive for the quality of the final drawing, which to some extent represents the visual evidence of the way the draughtsman has understood the object and the extent to which he is capable of developing a drawing systematically.

On pp. 25–27 are a number of examples showing various objects depicted with the aid of systematically drawn draft sketches of spatial envelopes. In every case one can recognize the attempt not do draw the actual form of contours and surfaces directly from the object, but to approach the final form by approximation via enveloping volumes.

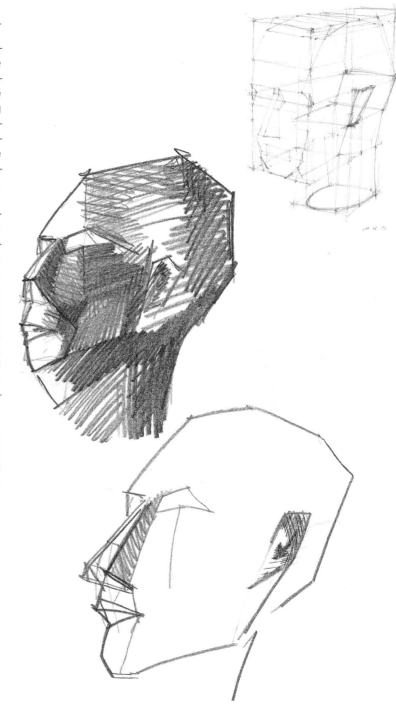

The form is developed from the enveloping volume by the articulation of adjoining surface planes.

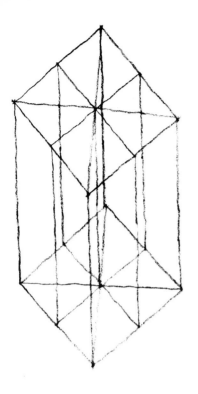
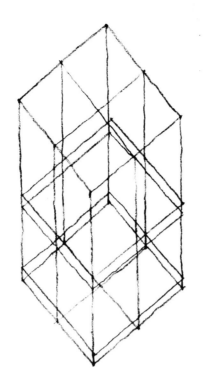
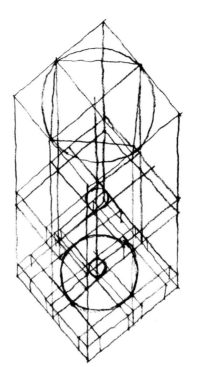
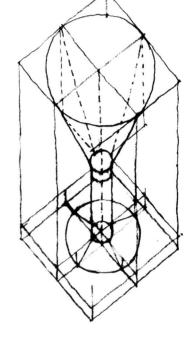

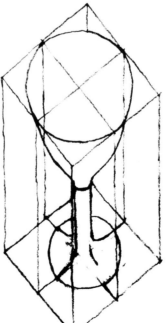

Examples of the depiction of simple
objects, using guide (construction) lines
and enveloping volumes.
1. Spatial envelope, vertical
2. Spatial envelope, horizontal
3. Insertion of outlines (at various levels)
4. Approximate form
5. Contours
6. Three-dimensional form

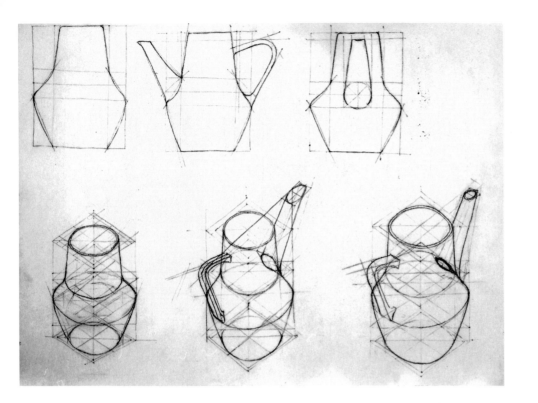

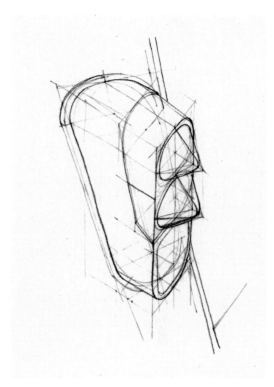

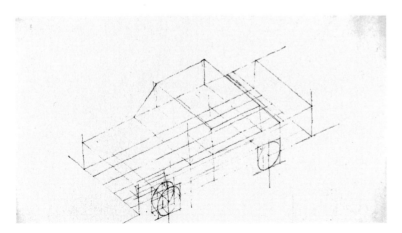

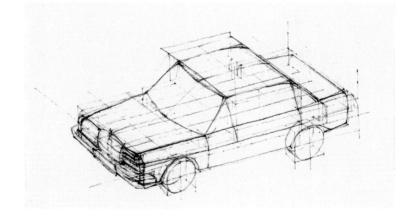

The sketches show that the technical process of drawing is basically an extremely simple one, if the proportional articulation is logically handled. The enclosing volumetric envelope and the object itself then retain their true relationship to each other. The imaginative faculty also undergoes an excellent training, since one has to visualize the object as transparent, as if it were made of glass (cf. p. 38).

Preliminary studies for the drawing on
the right. The church tower is depicted in
the form of a series of octagonal prisms
stacked on top of each other and having a
common central axis.

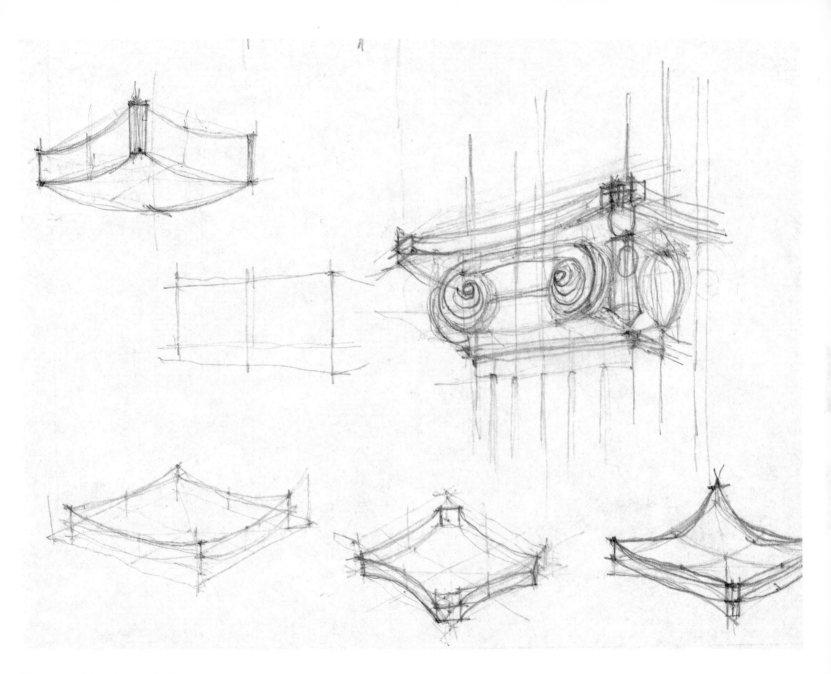

The abacus of the column capital is
developed from a flat slab, the corners of
which are turned up in the drawing. In
this way the drawing illustrates the
quality of three-dimensional distortion.

Spatial Relationships

The organs of equilibrium in our ears enable us to walk upright and permit us to differentiate between vertical and horizontal. As a result we come to perceive our surroundings in terms of top and bottom, front and back. The fact that spatial distortions occur in the process is usually only registered, when we see parallel straight lines converging and vanishing in the distance. One very rarely finds situations of this kind in nature. There the sense of space is conveyed on the one hand by the colours of the landscape (i.e. colours tend to pale with increasing distance), and on the other by the dissolution of details; (in a forest, for example, one can scarcely distinguish the individual trees).

In architecture, however, which is almost invariably based on geometric volumes, the impression of depth is extremely concrete. Although the edges of architectural objects follow oblique lines in space, our visual habits, in conjunction with the organs of equilibrium, convey the impression that we are looking at horizontal or vertical lines. Should this joint process of perception – via the organs of sight and balance – be impaired, a sense of giddiness will be felt with the well-known symptoms of vertigo and nausea (sea-sickness). We experience the same sensation on entering spaces with an oblique or distorted form of construction, as one sometimes finds at fairs. If the edges of a space are not parallel or at right angles to the force of gravity of the earth, the impression can be created, for example, that water is running uphill.

Perceptual delusions of this kind reveal the importance of correct spatial perception. As the illustration shows, a person's faculty for spatial vision may be underdeveloped. This is especially noticeable when it manifests itself in the form of a drawing. Spatial perception presupposes an awareness of the facts that true dimensions appear foreshortened in a spatial image, that surface areas appear in a distorted form, and that horizontal lines extend to vanishing points that lie above or below the height of the beginning of the line.

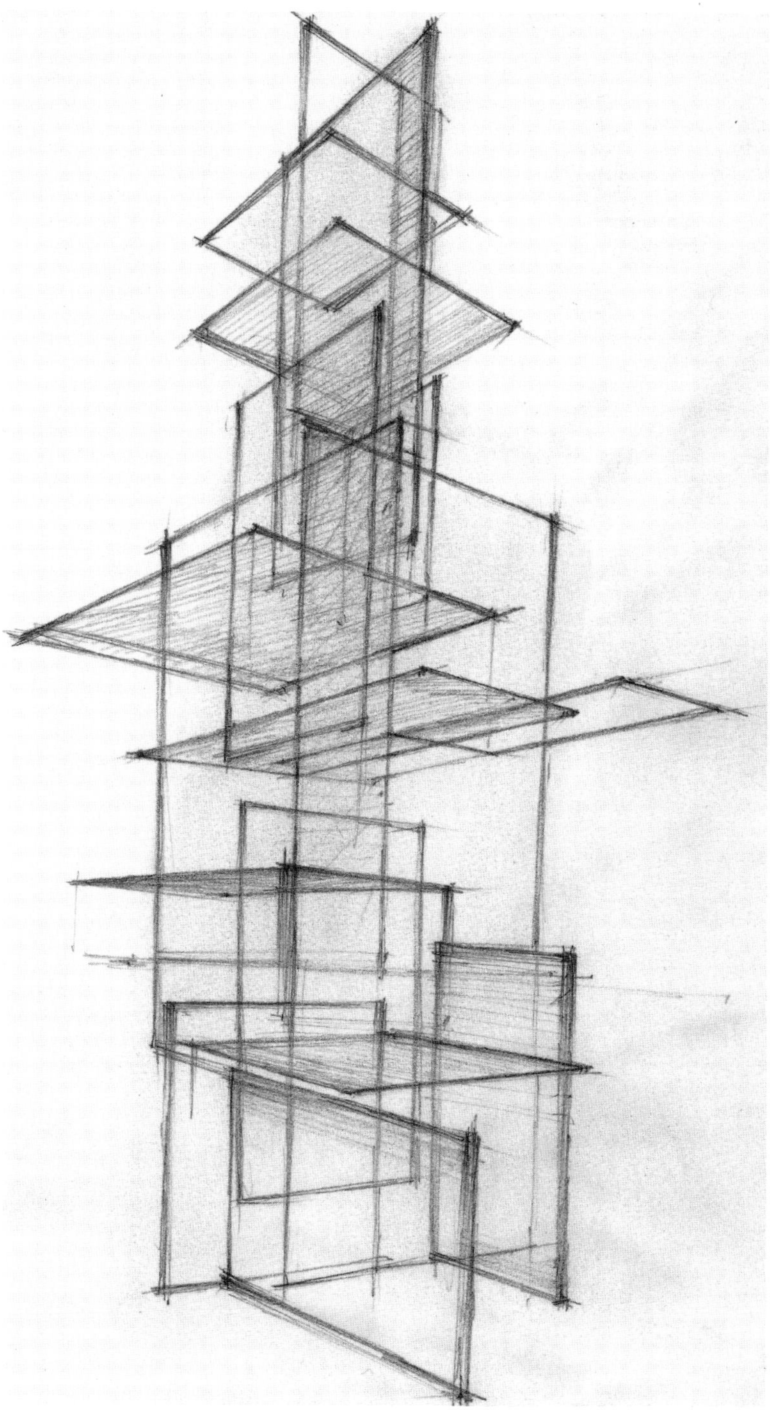

Unsuccessful attempt by an architectural student to draw an object in perspective.

Planes in space

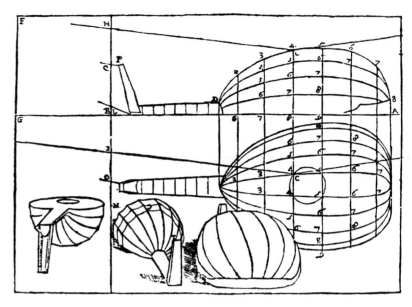

The musical instrument is depicted in
the form of a spatial network.

Albrecht Dürer demonstrating a
technique of perspective drawing using
a gridded screen.

As early as the 15th century gridded screens had been introduced as a device to facilitate the study of these phenomena. The contours of an object were followed within the grid and were recorded on gridded paper. This drawing technique is both logical and simple. All it requires of the draughtsman is an ability for precise observation. The object is reduced to a network of lines that approximate to the actual form. For the sake of simplicity and comprehension, we shall refer to this as the ›network method‹.

Drawing Using Comparative Reference Points (Network Method)

As mentioned above, the network method consists of observing the salient points of an object in their relative positions, recording these on paper, and joining them up with lines. One finds comparable examples of this in painting books for children, where a series of dots are enumerated and can be joined by a line to reveal the image of some familiar object.

A systematic description of this technique will be given, taking the street scene in Vézélay (pp. 34–35) as an example. The tower in the centre of the picture is without doubt a good starting point. The vertical edges of the houses and the eaves lines are further clearly recognizable elements of the picture. They are drawn in the form of linear structures. Having reached this stage, one can determine the positions of the tower windows, for example, from the vertical edge of the house on the right, marking them off with construction lines or dots. The other major elements in the picture can be dealt with in the same manner. The notation of vertical and horizontal lines of reference and comparison and the diagonal vanishing lines of roofs, eaves, etc. is particularly useful in this respect. Finally, ancillary components such as windows, walls, trees, etc. should be drawn in, until the spatial picture is complete.

This method never fails to succeed. It has one serious disadvantage, however. It does not stimulate spatial perception, since the three-dimensional quality of reality is apprehended neither mentally nor via the process of drawing. In other words, this method is a purely mechanical device for those who have to perfect their graphic technique before they can concentrate on the problem of spatial relationships.

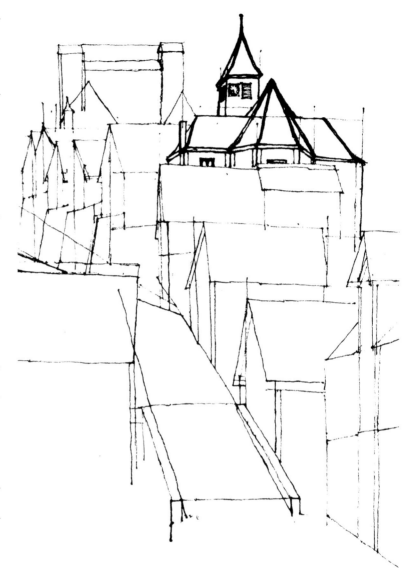

Example of a spatial sketch, built up by means of a system of comparative reference points.

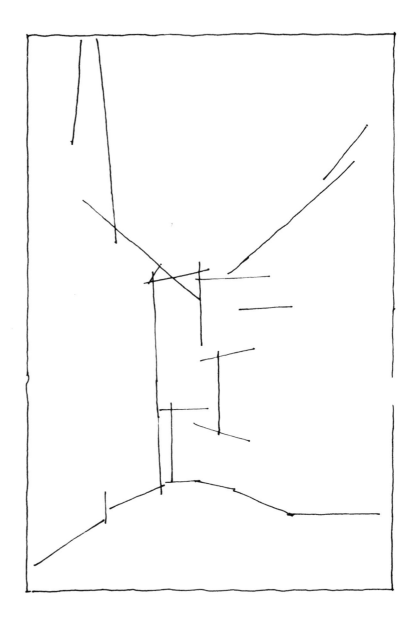

The technique described is demonstrated taking the street in Vézélay, shown in the photograph, as an example. The drawing is developed by means of comparative reference points.

Salient points are linked to each other by straight lines. Oblique lines are inserted.

34

Choice of reference points, establishing a series of vertical and horizontal co-ordinates.

From the network of construction lines and reference points the drawing begins to emerge as a copy of the actual spatial image.

35

Drawing According to the Laws of Perspective

If one wishes to draw spatial forms with precision, a knowledge of the laws of geometric perspective construction is necessary. According to these, all straight lines that are parallel to each other and parallel to the main line of vision (visual ray) have a common vanishing point at eye-level, i.e. on the so-called horizon line. Elements situated above the horizon are seen from below; those below the horizon line are seen from above. If one is not careful, a picture can appear to be drawn from a viewpoint where the draughtsman cannot possibly have stood; (e.g. 15 feet above street level). Although the drawing may appear to be correct, in terms of perspective it will be wrong; (see below).

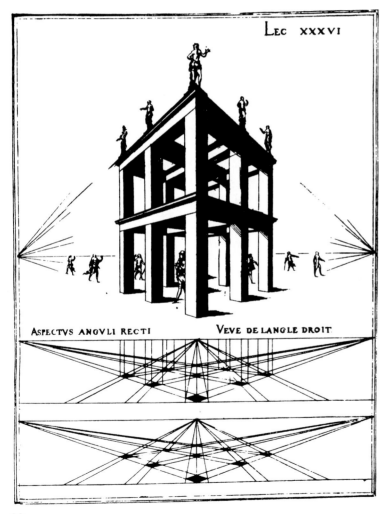

The level of the horizon line is indicated by the height (or eye level) of the persons standing at various points on the ground. The points of intersection of the lines extending from the edges of the volume indicate the vanishing points.

Construction of Perspective Image (Visual Ray Method)

1. The position of the picture plane (BE), the standpoint (S) and the distance (a) from the picture plane are determined on plan. The main visual ray (H) is at right angles to the picture plane.

2. The height (h) of the standpoint (viewpoint) should be marked off on the side elevation of the object.

3./4. Extend lines from the centre of projection (viewpoint) through all salient points of the object to intersect with the picture plane. Every point of the object thus has its counterpart (point of intersection) on the picture plane; (e.g. A → A').

5. The positions of the salient points of the object in the perspective image lie at the points of intersection of the parallel lines extended from the orthogonal picture plane projections of the plan and side elevation; (e.g. A'', D''). By joining these points together, one obtains the perspective image of the volume. In the case of objects of a complexer shape than the cube shown here, the number of salient points will have to be increased to obtain a sufficiently accurate perspective image.

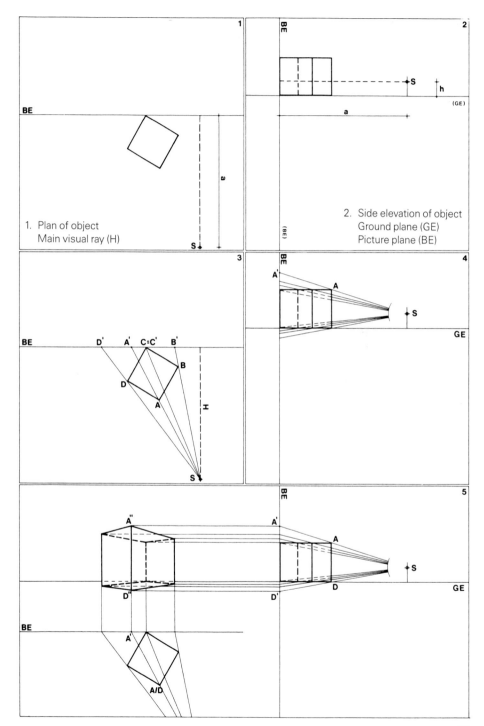

1. Plan of object
   Main visual ray (H)

2. Side elevation of object
   Ground plane (GE)
   Picture plane (BE)

In perspective drawing it is also important to depict the edges of an object that are not visible. This can only be done, if one imagines the object to be transparent, as if made of glass. We would then see not merely the surfaces turned towards us, but the faces at the rear as well. Projection lines should be extended through all major edges, etc. to their relevant vanishing points. In this way it will be possible to compare every part in its correct relationship to the others in a perspective layout. In contrast to the ›network method‹, one sees here that the draughtsman has to show conceptual ability in taking account of concealed parts of the object, and that it is necessary to go round the whole object mentally as part of the perceptual process. This stimulates the development of spatial perception and an understanding of transparency, plasticity and relief.

In terms of drawing technique one approaches the object in a manner similar to that of the network method, whereby salient features, like a street surface or the face of a house, can be drawn in perspective, and other parts of the picture related to these. But here too one should work consistently with vanishing lines, which are easily determined by taking bearings from the various oblique lines in the picture and sketching them in. If the vanishing points lie off the sheet of drawing paper (something that frequently occurs), one will have to be content with an approximate estimation of the angle of the vanishing lines.

Determining vanishing points on the basis of a plan sketch is not merely a long-winded process; in free-hand sketching it is out of all proportion to the purpose. Where a building has edges running in a number of different directions, one would have to construct a number of pairs of vanishing points. Inclined surfaces have their own vanishing points, which have to be taken into account as well (see p. 41). The angle of view should be assumed to be not greater than 30°, otherwise the outcome will be a kind of ›wide angle‹ drawing. This is often forgotten in the case of tall, towering buildings, with the result that the drawing conveys a false impression of the actual situation.

In practice it is generally advisable to begin with a preliminary perspective study to fix the spatial co-ordinates. Details can then be added in accordance with the network method. In drawing exercises one should start with simple objects that do not have a complex spatial construction (e.g. Romanesque churches). Later, however, one should systematically increase the degree of difficulty and try one's hand at complex spatial forms such as Baroque vaulting.

Spatial depiction with the aid of perspective construction. The guide lines along the walls and ceiling all converge at a central vanishing point.

Perspective stage construction. Magnificent princely palaces and statues with a
triumphal arch in the middle; perspective stage set for tragedies. To intensify the sense
of depth, the floor and walls were built to slope, (design by Serlio). This is a particularly
clear example of the way all parallel lines of a building converge on a single, central
vanishing point.

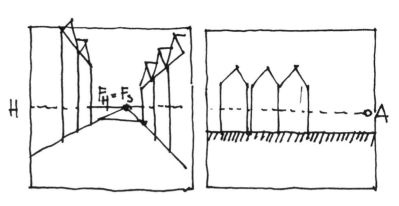

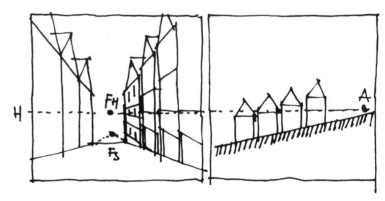

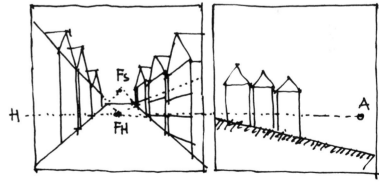

Special cases of perspective:
additional vanishing points for surfaces sloping up or down.
1. Level surfaces: vanishing points of road surface and building lines are identical.
2. Falling surfaces: the vanishing point for the road area (F_s) lies below the vanishing point for the lines of the buildings (F_h).
3. Rising surfaces: the vanishing point for the road area lies above the vanishing point for the lines of the buildings.

Perspective sketch   Elevation

The spatial impression is brought out by exaggerating the perspective.

Spatial sketch in which the form of the object has been changed during the drawing process. New forms were created by repeatedly drawing over the previous sketch. (Study in the monastery church of Rot an der Rot.)

43

Graphic Structures

Grey Tones

Up to now the drawing process has mainly been described in terms of line drawing. Every object has a surface with its own special characteristics, however. We shall therefore turn our attention now to the depiction of surface qualities and of light and shade by means of grey tones. The reproduction of grey tones is of fundamental importance, where one wishes to make the sculptural qualities of an object the central feature of a drawing. Since light and shade are fundamental to the visual effect, the choice of viewpoint has to take account of lighting conditions.

In reality every surface has its own coloration, which, in being reproduced in a drawing, has to be translated into a tone of grey. To sharpen one's awareness of this, it is worthwhile studying the grey tones of black and white photographs. One will notice that it is possible to distinguish the finest gradations of grey tone. Furthermore, one will come to see that the edges of objects are not defined by dark lines, but that the sense of plasticity is created by light and dark shades and contrasts. As a rule it should be possible to create a grey-tone drawing without contour lines.

Linear and grey-tone drawings

44

Stippling and Hatching

By building up and overlaying graphic structures one can achieve various stippled and hatched shading effects. Both techniques are important and need to be discussed in detail. Although all techniques can be used in conjunction with each other, we shall divide them up here into stippling, parallel and free-hand hatching, in order to discuss them more clearly.

Stippling. Having set out the spatial relationships and articulation of an object in a simple preliminary sketch, the various areas can then be shaded with a series of fine dots. The draft sketch should be drawn quite faintly, so that the surfaces of a volume will not be defined by contour lines but by areas of grey. The first stage of the work is to cover the entire surface of the object with an even, dotted shading. In further stages the areas that are to be darker will be toned down by further stippling, if necessary to the point where the entire surface of the paper is covered and a black area is created.

With this technique one has the whole range of grey-tones at one's command – from light to dark. The procedure is a slow one and should be undertaken step by step. The drawing acquires a static, technical character.

Various stippled textures

Parallel hatching. In principle hatched shading can consist of long or short strokes. Parallel hatching is typified by the homogeneity of the line structure and the resulting grey tone. If more than one layer of hatching is applied, overlaid on top of each other, one will logically obtain a similar progressive darkening of tone to that achieved with stippling. Depending on the form of depiction desired, parallel hatching can be in two directions that cross each other; the areas of hatching can abut or overlap each other and have different angles of line. The grey tones thus obtained are usually of a somewhat sterile appearance. In depicting flat surfaces, as in architecture, this may be appropriate; but in the case of sculpturally moulded or convoluted surfaces (e.g. landscapes) it can be problematic, since the expressive quality of this form of shading is limited.

Various layers of parallel hatching
(Morandi): short parallel hatching; lines
abutting and overlapping.

Parallel hatching: areas of shading
abutting and overlaid.

Various forms of parallel hatching

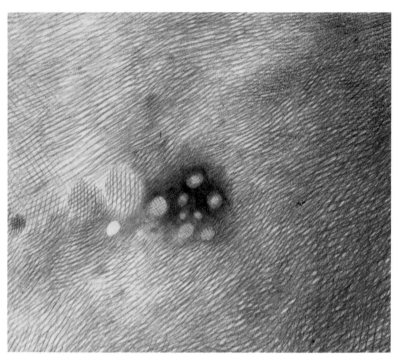

Free-hand Shading. A typical form of free-hand shading consists of curving lines of different thickness and direction and of variable spacing. With this shading technique it is possible to give expression to objects of complex sculptural shape und surface quality.

The flexibility of the linear network allows one to create light and dark tonal values relatively simply, especially where a number of layers of shading are applied. Areas that are kept extremely light in tone, including unshaded areas of white paper surrounded by areas of darker hatching, can help to bring out the plastic surface quality of an object. Since this drawing technique enables one to achieve the highest degree of expression, the initial steps described and illustrated here should be practised systematically, taking simple examples. To help perfect one's technique, original drawings of recognized quality should be studied (e.g. in the print and drawing departments of museums).

Curved line shading dissolving in density from dark to light. (Top: Georg Muche; bottom: Rembrandt.)

Charles Rennie Mackintosh: Inn at Fortingall. Drawing using various types of shading
without contour lines.

Depiction of an architectural object using a network of superimposed layers of shading
to bring out the filigrane character of the architecture; (Nevers Cathedral, Burgundy).

Shading resolved into a series of dense and less dense layers, consisting of various patterns of free-hand lines. It is not so much a depiction of the architecture that is created here as an interpretation of the spatial mood.

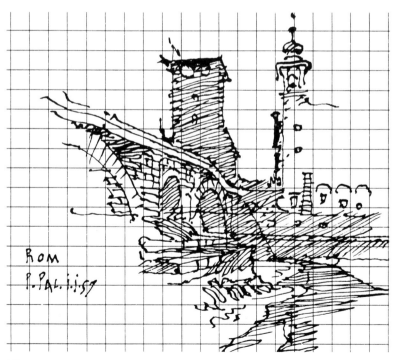

Examples of different shading techniques, the line qualities of which reveal quite distinct and individual styles of drawing.
Top left: Otto Ubbelohde, ca. 1910.
Top right: Canaletto, St. Mark's Square, ca. 1727.

Left: Hans Döllgast's personal and characteristic style of drawing. The hatched lines are not broken off at the ends, but drawn over the object in a continous layer. The grey tones are not strongly differentiated, a circumstance that reduces the sculptural quality of the object; (ca. 1959).

Right: Line drawing and areas of free-hand shading juxtaposed; (Rudi Hradil, Bridge, 1975).

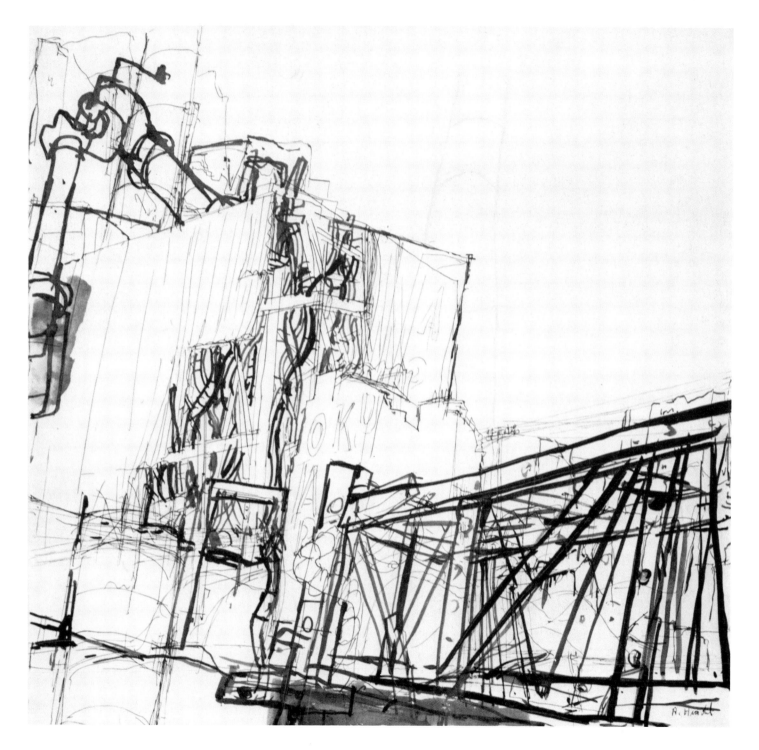

Heightening in White

If one draws on grey or other tinted paper, in addition to the possibility of toning down with layers of shading, one has scope to create lighter spots by applying white pigments (white pencil, crayon, etc.). The technique is referred to as heightening in white or high-lighting and represents an extension of the range of plastic expression in drawing.

A similar effect can be achieved by removing pigment from a darkly shaded area by means of a rubber.

An alternative technique is to darken the relevant areas of the paper with graphite dust and then to structure them with shading. In this way one can achieve a drawing with various tonal densities of grey, from which white high-lights can be picked out with the sharp tip of a rubber. By drawing in further details or shading and renewed erasure, graphic effects of great density and high quality can be achieved.

Spatial effects and plasticity can by achieved by traces of erasure.
Sketch, high-lighted with white crayon.

Graphic density achieved by repeated shading and high-lighting of parts of the drawing.
Academy Theatre in Mantua.

Representation of Surface Properties and Qualities of Materials

With the skilful use of grey tones it is possible to give expression to the surface character of different materials in a drawing. This demands considerable proficiency in drawing, however, since great precision is necessary. The depiction of surface properties is achieved by the creation of the appropriate graphic structures, and in this respect one must distinguish between sharp or smudged, light or dark dots, long and short lines, and various kinds of shading and layering effects. Surface character can reflect the rough state of a material (structure) or its artistic treatment in a dressed state (facture). It can appear rough and mat or smooth and polished. Light reflexes and mirror-like reflections can make a decisive contribution to the accurate legibility of surface character. Where very finely graded grey tones are to be employed, the drawing should be set out to a large scale. Graphic structures that may be recognizable at close quarters (e.g. 6-8 inches) tend to dissolve at a normal viewing distance (e.g. 3 feet) into a seemingly homogeneous, perfectly even grey tone. This visual phenomenon is often used in the realm of graphic design. The fineness of execution and the quality of the craftsmanship can be further heightened by photographing the drawing and reducing it in size. Virtual perfection with effects of this kind can be achieved by using a spray gun.

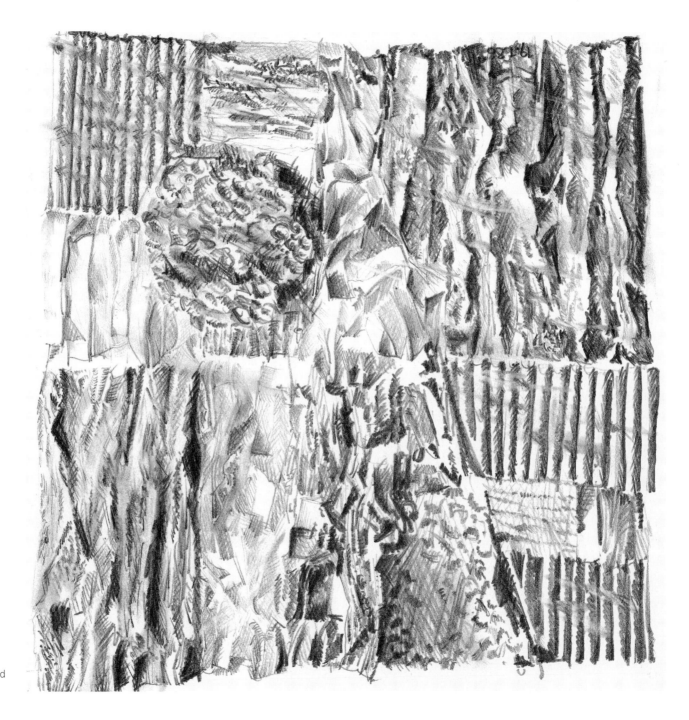

Sketch showing various
surface textures. Relief and
material

Shadow Effects

Shadows are a fundamental element of three-dimensional effect. In a drawing it is possible to make this particular aspect a central feature of the depiction. If one observes areas of shadow, one will notice that any volume appears darker on the faces turned away from the light. This is known as contained shadow. In addition, a volume also casts a shadow on the surfaces adjacent to it, provided that the source of light is not too diffuse. This is referred to as cast shadow. Both kinds of shadow are important for an accurate depiction of an object.

In a drawing the outlines of the areas of shadow are sketched in by means of fine construction lines and the appropriate grey tone shaded in. The boundary lines of the area of shadow should never be darker than the tone of the shaded area itself, nor should they be allowed to appear as distinct lines; otherwise the effect of plasticity created by the shadow will be lost. As the adjacent sketches show, shadow effects can help to create a ›positive‹ image of an object (with a lighter background), or a ›negative‹ image (where the background is darker). Within the area of contained shadow one can, as a rule, recognize certain surface characteristics; this may also occasionally be the case within the area of cast shadow.

Shadow studies.
Left hand page: different shadow effects. Cast and contained shadow (left); shadows of Inca ruins brought out in a strong contrast photocopy of a photograph (right).
This page, left: relief by Oskar Schlemmer.

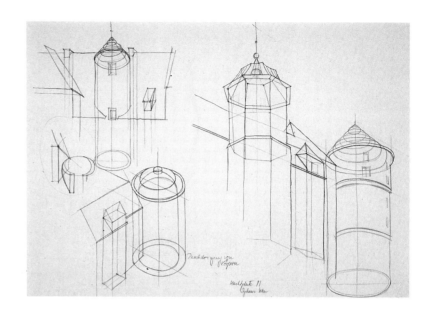

A sense of plasticity created by shadows.
Above: preliminary sketch to show interpenetration of volumes.
Below: three-dimensionality of form brought out not by drawn outlines, but by areas of shading.

Landscape by Rembrandt. Panoramic view of Haarlem with Saxenburg (ca. 1650).
What is striking here is the high degree of simplification, the simple means with which
the character of the landscape is reproduced.

Trees, Landscapes, Ensembles

Anyone who is acquainted with Johann Wolfgang von Goethe's description of his »Italian Journey« will be aware that at that time drawing played an important role in the context of social communication. Although Goethe was receptive to the distinguishing features of a landscape, his travel sketches are more a documentation of his emotional and romantic experience. It was not sober, analytical observation that was paramount to him, but the need to capture surroundings he felt to be beautiful and romantic.

This habit, this romantic point of view, has endured to this day. Southern villages, fishing boats and narrow, twisting lanes in old towns are the favourite subjects for travel sketches. One might justifiably question the motivation for drawing any travel sketch; but there is no point in criticizing the phenomenon, since it is based on an emotional urge that one is not in a position to discuss here.

It is possible, on the other hand, to take a critical look at the quality of the draughtsmanship in the depiction of landscapes, trees and indeed human figures. Ignoring the purely naturalistic element of such representations, one of the main features of a drawing, in contrast to photography, is its ability to capture the essential character of a spatial situation or an object. Implicit to this is the ability to sketch landscapes, trees, human figures, etc. in a succinct but felicitous manner.

Landscapes

The first thing one has to heed in drawing a landscape is the overall spatial composition. Flat, undulating, folding or layered areas should be seen as a formal expression and translated accordingly into drawing. The second important aspect is the differentiation between forms in the foreground, middle-distance and background. Just as the ability of the eye to resolve objects into their individual parts diminishes with increasing distance, so analogously, background objects should be depicted in a simplified manner. By allowing lines to dissolve, by simplifying contours and at the same time creating areas of greater density, one can convey an impression of depth and distance. Above all it is essential to draw from nature.

LE BEAUSET
Solei 86

Trees

One should begin by observing how trees differ considerably in their basic forms and in the nature of their growth. It is therefore useful to study bare trees initially. Outlines of their skeletal forms should be drawn, showing the dimensions and directions of the various parts in relationship to each other. Even when drawing trees with their foliage, it is important and of great help to sketch this structure in a draft study. In addition to increasing the precision of the outline, the details of the top of the tree should be elaborated in linear form in further stages of the work. Finally, the plasticity of the whole should be brought out by the insertion of areas of shading. One should not overlook the fact that a tree almost never possesses a thick black circular outline. If one is interested purely in the basic form of a tree, it is important to find the right balance of accuracy of detail and simplification. This can only be achieved by an intense·study of nature.

Depictions of trees reduced to overall form and basic characteristics of growth.

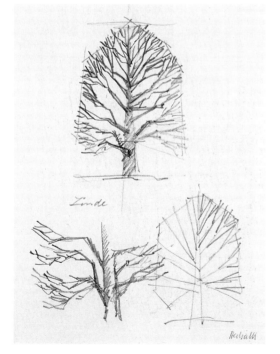

62

Various degrees of elaboration of the characteristics of trees: density and transparency.

Human Figures and Animals

Drawing human beings is a difficult exercise. The reason for this lies in the different appearances and the complex shapes of people. Without adequate studies from the nude, one will never be able to comprehend the true sets of physical relationships; the outcome of this are amorphous, clumsy forms such as those in the sketch on the left. If the drawing is to be of a higher quality, it is necessary to develop the size and form of the human body with the aid of enveloping volumes and construction lines. The actual form of the body can indeed be sketched beneath the clothes initially. In addition the statics and dynamics of the human body are important – the way people stand, sit, walk, etc. Gestures of movement of this kind can be captured relatively easily in the form of a simplified cubic depiction. Drawings such as these can also be corrected more easily – something that is necessary, as a rule. The drawing has to show the correct distribution of weight and forces in the body, otherwise the impression of a stiff, cramped posture will be given, even in simplified depictions. Finally, one should not overlook the importance of proportions. What is decisive in this context is whether the type of figure is tall and thin or short and stocky.

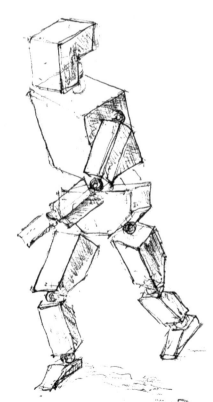

In terms of drawing technique, it is easier to portray human figures and animals, if the form is drawn with a ›searching‹ line that is subject to correction. The more simply the basic features of any particular posture are captured, the greater will be the quality of the drawing.

The Nature of Architectural Drawing

The invention of the felt-tip pen has proved to be disastrous for architectural sketching. The problem with this implement is its bold, even, black line quality that immediately fixes contours and virtually obviates a ›searching‹ style of drawing. It is almost impossible to differentiate between light and heavy, thick or thin lines. As a result of this, drawings made with felt-tip implements usually lack a sense of lightness and personal touch. If, in addition, large areas of the drawing are shaded with sterile parallel hatching, one has taken the step from individuality to mediocre graphics, which only possess any life at all through their subtle placement of lines, and which quickly become uninteresting.

In the process of perfecting one's skills as a draughtsman, the thematic content of one's drawings should come to assume precedence. In other words, the draughtsman should no longer select his subjects merely according to emotional or romantic criteria, but with a view to reflecting the characteristics of a particular place or a particular type of object. In order to ascertain what these are, it is necessary to consider, before starting to draw, what one intends to depict. One might attempt, for example, as in the picture on the left, to achieve an accurate, factual portrayal of an American street; or it might be certain formal qualities, such as the ornamentation of a church (as in the drawing on the right) that one wishes to express. A drawing with thematic content will no longer seek merely to reproduce a particular image; it will attempt to convey the draughtsman's own interpretation of a situation. This whole issue will be examined in greater depth in the following sections. (Cf. illustrations on p. 83.)

Analytical Drawing

Over and above its technical and depictive aspects, the architectural drawing can assume a greater significance in an analytical role. The analytical process in drawing, rather like that involved in chemical analysis, consists of reducing the architectural object as a whole to its constituent parts: order (proportions), form (plasticity) and decoration (ornamentation). On the basis of an actual pictorial analysis, an attempt will be made to demonstrate the basic features of analytical thinking in a comparative form.

Picture Analysis

In addition to the statement it makes (subject, meaning), every pictorial product can be studied analytically according to its compositional features. Even where the actual outcome of compositional activity is extremely complex in form, certain basic relationships can be identified. As the broken piece of rock in the illustration on the left shows, even nature divulges certain compositional features. The picture is divided up by bold lines, which lead to the formation of greater and lesser node points. In other words, hierarchies are established by means of planar sections, directional elements and interlocking, network-like structures. The analytical sketches based on this do no more than record these features.

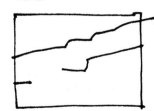

Hierarchy: centres and sub-centres (node points).

Planar divisions, directions and networks.

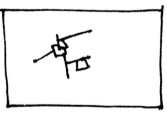
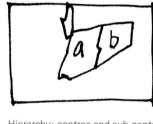

The following three examples of actual painted scenes quite clearly reveal the following characteristics: constriction to an aperture-like form, convergence of lines towards a vanishing point, and a grid-like structure. In addition, one can identify the individual compositional elements (e.g. the rocks, trees, human figures, buildings, paths, areas of water and the sky). This ordering system of co-ordinates has to be looked for behind the immediate impression conveyed by the pictorial themes. For analytical purposes one therefore quite deliberately divides the picture as a whole into a series of layers, so that each can be studied on its own. In terms of the drawing process that means bringing out the features that have been isolated in this way and making them visible.

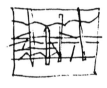

In abstract painting the compositional features sometimes manifest themselves quite simply, as for example in the picture »Jolie Eva« by Picasso. The analytical drawing reveals an ordering framework consisting of divisions, directional elements and proportions. The picture can slowly be decoded in this way. For a deeper understanding of the work, it is necessary to turn to the history of art. The same of course applies to the analysis of architecture.

In this context the architectural drawing comes to assume an exceptional significance. Neither photographs nor film can provide anything like the same degree of access to the formal design qualities of a work as analytical drawing can. The graphic content is not concerned with a purely three-dimensional spatial representation; it seeks to provide a statement that may well be in shorthand form, but which is all the more precise in its expression of individual isolated qualities. Graphic aesthetics recede into the background; thematic content comes to the fore.

An analytical sketch reveals the compositional principles underlying the picture. Planar subdivisions and directional elements are brought out.

The graphical elaboration of the drawing trains the eye to perceive surface qualities.

Architectural Analysis – Analytical Drawing

The main purpose of analytical architectural drawing is to discover the design qualities of a building. The drawing will therefore not concern itself with emotional atmosphere but with the rational facts underlying the object in its manifold entirety. The purpose of the analysis is to reveal the features of the design in isolation. This process leads to a new synthesis and helps to simplify and prepare the ground, through the medium of drawing, for the invention of new forms.

Axes/Geometrical Order

As described previously, in analysing architecture, we can assume that, with few exceptions, the composition of a building will largely consist of geometric planes and volumes. The purpose of the analytical drawing is therefore to extract this (assumed) ordering concept from the object as a whole and to depict it in an approximate manner.

The first step in this systematic process concerns the primary systems of articulation or subdivision (e.g. axes of symmetry). In this context there are a number of different factors one has to take into account. A building may be

Chambord: entrance face; earlier stage of design. Closer observation shows that, in its detailed form and in the articulation of the façade, the building is quite asymmetrical.

73

laid out about a clear central axis, but at the same time have an underlying ordering system that, although appearing to be symmetrical, is in fact not strictly regular; (e.g. Chambord). Axes of symmetry may also recur at regular or irregular intervals. An analytical drawing will seek to identify these ordering systems and depict them as a series of axes or in grid form (e.g. a, a, a/ a, b, a/a, b, c, b, a, etc.)

Articulating systems of this kind can be based on horizontal as well as vertical axes and they can be drawn in isolation as distinct elements of the design. This is only possible, however, when the draughtsman has developed the ability, not merely to see the form of an object, but to recognize the underlying ordering system as well. It is necessary therefore to comprehend

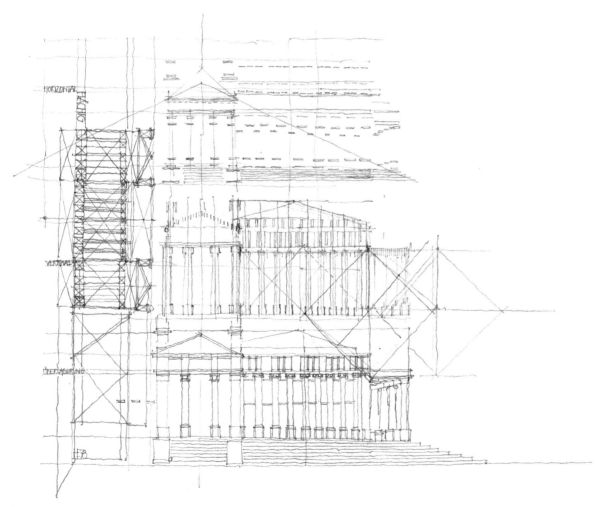

Analytical studies of a rhythmically structured architectural object; (Königsbau, Stuttgart). From top to bottom one sees the following analytical stages: horizontal, vertical, combined; on plan (left).

the sets of relationships described here. The drawing will usually take the form of an orthogonal system of axes (with all its ramifications) representing the order underlying the articulation of the façade.

The examples illustrated here are analyses based on axes of symmetry and on horizontal and vertical articulation. Mirror images and identifiable regular divisions are depicted by a technique of simple linear graphics.

The two diagrams below illustrate the sequence followed in the drawing. In the first sketch vertical and horizontal divisions and the outer geometric envelopes are drawn in the form of triangles and rectangles. This represents the first stage of the analysis. The second sketch shows the elaboration of the façade drawing. The subordinate forms are located initially in the right-hand half. These remain visible as a linear framework in the detailed sketch in the left-hand half.

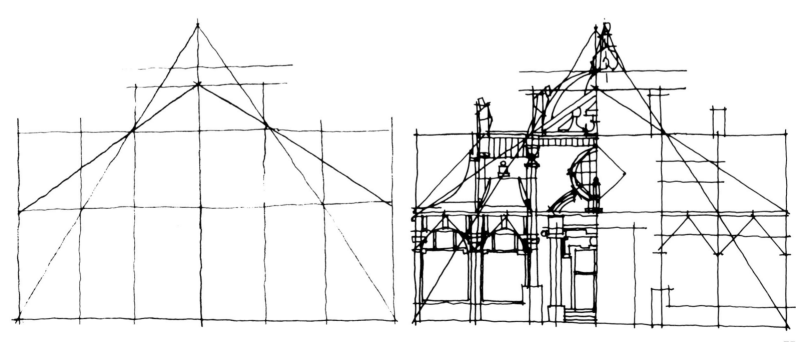

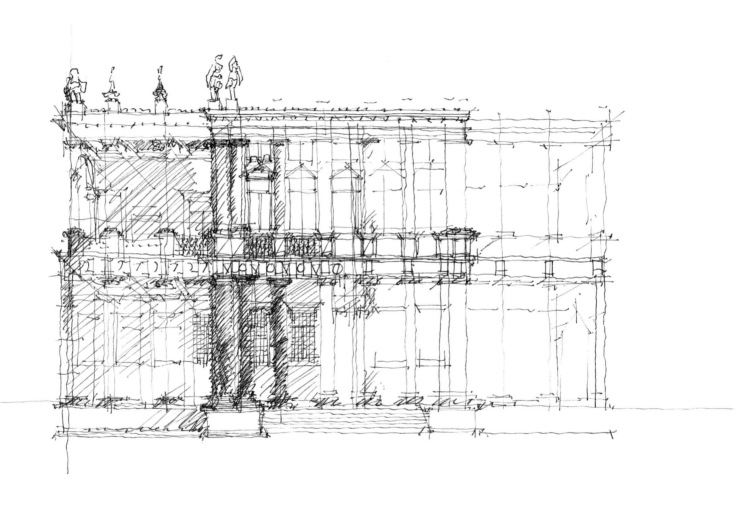

Palazzo Chiericati, Vicenza. Combination of analytical elements in a single drawing:
vertical and horizontal articulation, major and minor forms.

Plane Surfaces

Having established the axial divisions of a building, the analysis can move on to consider a further aspect: the size and position of planar subdivisions. A façade can be interpreted, analogously to its axial articulation, as a system of vertical and horizontal planes, which may abut or overlap. In this analytical process it is essential not to allow oneself to be distracted by the sculptural ornamentation of a building, for the very purpose of this is to disguise the underlying ordering relationships one is looking for here. Similarly, pronounced relief in a façade can complicate the search for planar divisions.

It is quite possible that a number of observers will come to different conclusions in their analyses, since analytical skills and visual habits vary. This element of subjectivity cannot be excluded. It can only be reduced by a close examination of the object itself.

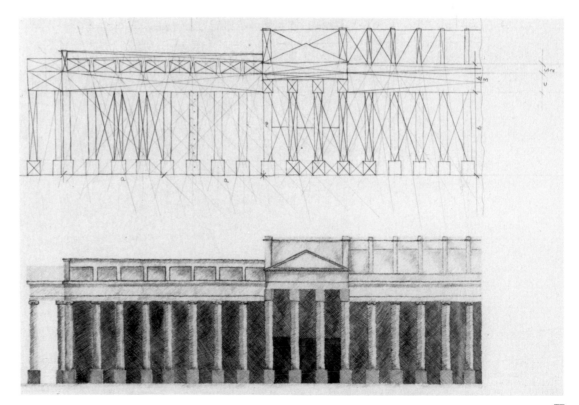

Drawings analysing planar articulation. The form of the object is dominated by vertical and horizontal planes; (Königsbau, Stuttgart; cf. p. 74).

Proportions

Having established the axes and planar articulation of a building, the next stage is the estimation of the relative proportions. It is no longer sufficient to record spacings and the sizes of the various surface planes. These now have to be integrated into a system of proportions, by which the smaller units should be related to the larger ones. The purpose of this is to ascertain, where possible, according to what proportional relationships the object was designed. This is only possible, if one can select a viewpoint from which no perspective foreshortening of the object occurs. Information gained in previous analytical stages can help to establish proportional ordering systems based on squares, triangles or, on occasion, the Golden Section.

In this context Jakob Burckhardt refers to a concept of »harmonic« design, in which related planar proportions recur in vertical and horizontal forms in a façade. Applied to the design process, this suggests that it is not so much the dimensions of a building in feet or metres that are of significance, but the relationship of the parts to each other and to the whole.

Even if the precision of free-hand drawing has its limits and actual geometric measurement would lead to more accurate results, the value of this analytical stage lies in achieving an awareness of the underlying design process.

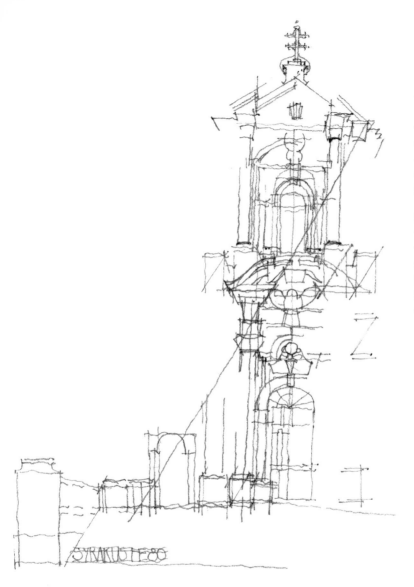

The diagonal construction lines reveal that the plane surfaces are related in scale; they also shed some light on the proportions of the building. Left: façade of Syracuse Cathedral; right: house fronts facing on to the Campo in Siena.

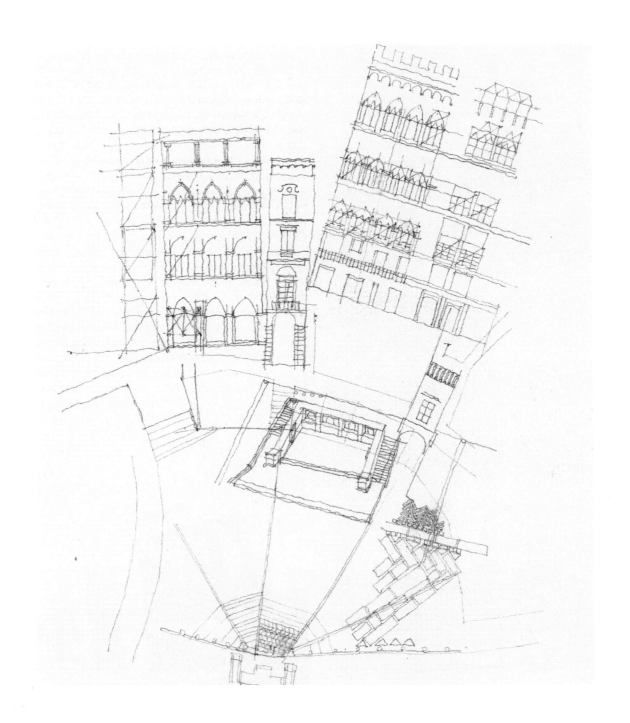

Three-Dimensional Processes

Continuing the analytical steps we have considered so far, it would seem only logical to extrapolate the principles governing the design of a façade and apply them to the overall three-dimensional form of the building. That would mean investigating whether the façade of the building is merely a mask, or whether the order found in the elevation is continued throughout the building in three-dimensional form. If, for example, the façade is composed of a series of planar elements, one might ask whether these are given three-dimensional expression in the overall design of the structure. It is the task of the analytical drawing to represent these relationships in a pictorial manner, whereby the actual shapes created in such three-dimensional processes can be extremely complex. In some situations one will encounter a certain ambiguity in the built form; but even here it is important that the analysis should recognize certain basic elements and functions such as support, abutment, pivoting, penetration, enclosure or cladding, layering and form-giving (moulding), and be able to depict these in a functional (i.e. reduced, succinct) manner. Alongside the mental process, the draughtsman has to develop a form of representation that, in addition to depicting actual shapes, expresses above all the *idea* behind what he has seen. The illustrations shown here are meant to demonstrate that it is possible to capture these characteristics in a kind of shorthand abbreviated form. With greater facility a personal style of drawing will manifest itself. The manner of drawing resembles that of a design sketch and at this level reveals the close intellectual relationship between analysis and synthesis.

In the drawings on the left-hand side of the next page one sees the development of three-dimensional spatial forms, e.g. intersection and interpenetration of volumes.
On the right: brief, sketched notations of three-dimensional processes. Not so much the form as the idea is conveyed by these drawings.

Architectural Motifs

In addition to exhibiting the special features we have already described, buildings are distinguished by certain characteristic formal motifs. These may manifest themselves in terms of repetition and rhythm, or they may be found in an ornamental system overlaying the basic order. They may determine the character of a single building or an entire street space. The drawings depict these features with a kind of graphic abbreviation that does not describe the exact details, but brings out the formal patterns and themes.

Library and Logetta, Venice. Detail showing the rhythmic sequence of formal elements: plinth, column, balcony, capital, cornice, crowning details.

Street in Gdansk (Danzig). The density of ornamental architectural forms is translated into a rhythmic sequence of grid-like lines.

Nevers Cathedral, Burgundy. The ornamental forms of the Gothic tower are depicted as a series of graphic patterns. The information they communicate is retained in the drawing.

Logetta del Capitano, Vicenza. The drawing shows the sequences of formal elements both vertically and horizontally.

Coloured Pencil (Crayon) Technique

The use of coloured pencils or crayons in drawing represents a further extension of the graphic techniques described so far. There is obviously a close relationship to hatching and shading on the one hand, and on the other, it is but a short step to painting, in terms of colour reproduction. That is why drawing with coloured pencils, crayons, etc. is regarded as a good preparation for water-colour painting.

The essential feature of painting is an ability to think in terms of coloured surfaces. This represents a fundamental difference from drawing, which demands a far more linear, contour-like form of perception. As a rule painting will therefore be concerned with the question of the coloration and colour transitions of a particular subject. This relationship cannot be emphasized strongly enough.

By inference, the underlying skill of painting consists of a knowledge of colours and how to mix them. The first step in this process is to analyse the coloration of one's surroundings. Whereas homogeneous colour relationships usually prevail in the case of artificially produced objects such as buildings, in the realm of nature one is almost invariably confronted with transitions from one colour to another. Both these phenomena can be reproduced with the appropriate skills and techniques.

Mixing Processes

There are basically two ways of mixing colours. One can either apply the desired shade of colour directly to the backing, in which case it has to be mixed beforehand; or one can obtain the tone one requires by mixing different colours on the actual surface to be treated. In the former case, when using paint, the colours will be mixed on a palette and applied to the relevant surface. If one is using coloured pencils this process has already been undertaken by the manufacturers in terms of the wide and finely graded range of colours they offer. In the latter case the mixing of colours takes place on the actual surface to be treated. Successive layers of colour should allow the layer below to shine through, thus creating the impression of a colour transition. Anyone who has studied the paintings of the Pointillists and Impressionists at close-quarters will easily be able to understand this transitional effect. From a distance one sees cohesive areas of colour; from close-to these dissolve into a myriad of small brush strokes of various shades. It is precisely this effect that is created in coloured pencil technique.

Single-Colour Tone: Light and Heavy Shading

It is a useful exercise to take a single colour and apply a number of layers of shading in such a way that the intensity ranges from dense to light. When the surface of the paper is completely covered with pigment, further intensification is only possible by applying greater pressure to the pencil.

Multi-Colour Tones: Colour Mixing

It is a simple process to blend colours by mixing and overlaying areas of coloured shading. New mixed tones are created in the process that differ from the original colours of the pencils or crayons used. One should be aware of the fact that the mixing of colours can also lead to a change in character (from bright to dull).

By copying a model (colour composition by Baumeister) the make-up of the colours can be discovered and reproduced using coloured pencils.

April 85
Mathias
Poetzmann
1235175

Studies from nature using coloured
pencil technique.

Colour Relationships

The various tones achieved by mixing are related to each other by virtue of the fact that they come about through the joint action of the original individual pigments. It is thus possible to create harmonious colour series.

Certain colours are not compatible with each other, however. This applies both to the brighter colours and to the grey and black tones; for example, when grey-brown is set alongside blue-grey. Based on a knowledge of colour contrasts, one has to develop an eye for the tensions that can arise between certain colours. Not merely will the luminosity of a colour be accentuated or dulled; its quality of warmth or coolness can also change, depending on the colours with which it is juxtaposed. In this respect one is urgently recommended to study the coloration of existing paintings and to experiment as much as possible oneself.

Schematic examples of cold and warm, bright and dull colour tones – the outcome of mixing (cf. p. 98).

Application: Architectural Depictions

Architecture largely consists of compositions of plane surfaces, with the result that one usually finds homogeneous surface colour values. These can generally be reproduced relatively simply with coloured pencils or crayons, since one has a precise control over the application of the colour. Technically speaking, one merely has to take care that the individual layers of coloured shading are applied with a sharply pointed pencil or crayon as homogeneously as possible, until one reaches the point where the individual strokes are no longer visible. If the colour value turns out to be too bright, the luminosity can be toned down with a layer of grey shading. Once the entire surface of the paper is covered with pigment, one may find that further layers of colour will not adhere, since there is no surface friction any more. All one can do in such cases is employ even softer pencils or use paper with a rougher surface texture on future occasions.

Water-Colour Technique

It is not the aim of this book to elevate any particular technique or form of representation to the status of a model. The underlying intention is to discuss those criteria with which the beginner must be familiar, in order to find a path for himself, via his own exercises, to a personal form of expression in drawing or painting. Many traditional schools of painting hinder a person's development to a state of independence with well intended advice that unfortunately places too great an emphasis on the question of naturalistic representation. Capturing the form of an object is certainly important; but it is much more important to show a pupil that form is not the sole or indeed the principal feature of painting. Coloration and the expression it communicates are at least as important.

Anyone who begins to comprehend this relationship will come to experience how his or her visual perception concentrates more and more on the coloration of an object and less and less on the form. The ability to »see« is augmented by a new dimension, and for the sensitive observer every painting will communicate new insights, not merely into the subject matter, but into the painterly treatment as well. The reader is therefore urged to study as many pictures as he can in museums and galleries and to develop his own emotional likes and dislikes relating to coloration and the nature of depiction, so that he may gradually realize his own personal abilities of expres-

Copy of a work by Picasso. (Cf. ill. p. 72.)

sion. Of course one starts off by admiring certain models and learns a great deal about painting technique and composition from attempting to copy them. There is no overlooking the fact that Macke and Mackintosh (architecture), Turner and Corot (landscape), and early Picasso (composition) all served as models for the illustrations on the following pages. One should remain open to inspiration of this and a similar kind, in order that the thematic treatment of a picture may become the ultimate aim and not mere technical skills.

The following sections should be understood in the light of the foregoing. After providing the essential technical information, we shall attempt to show that the first steps in coloured drawing can be followed by a liberation from a naturalistic view of things, thus opening the way for a personal form of expression in painting.

Implements and Materials

One should not select the cheapest product when purchasing water-colours, for the quality of the pigment may well be inferior. This will only become apparent later with actual use. Pigments may be mixed, which tends to impair their purity and leads to dull colour tones. Boxes of paints with 12 different colours, available from specialist dealers, provide a good range for initial requirements. All one will need to buy subsequently to complement these are ochre tones, which it is difficult to create by mixing.

When purchasing paper, it is sufficient to test it with the flat of the hand. If it feels cool to the touch, it has a smooth, low-absorbent surface and is not to be recommended for the beginner. If it does not have this cool effect, the surface texture will be somewhat rougher and more absorbent and thus easier to paint upon. At all events, the beginner should accustom himself to using one sort of paper, where the absorbent qualities are known. Changes of temperature are a further practical factor that has to be taken into account, for it makes a considerable difference whether one is painting indoors or using water-colours in the sun at 85°F. In the latter case the painted surfaces will dry out very quickly, with the result that one either has to paint more swiftly or use more water. For outdoor work one needs a small vessel to hold water. Sometimes it may be attached to the water-colour box; (consult specialist dealer). A small cloth of absorbent material is needed to dab off excess moisture or unsuccessful portions of the painting. Good quality water-colour brushes of badger or marten hair are very expensive. One can initially confine oneself to the sizes 2, 6 and 10. In the case of cheaper products one should check before purchase, whether the tip of the brush becomes soft in a wetted state, and whether the bristles retain their tension and return to a pointed form after bending. This physical property is necessary to distribute the paint over the surface of the paper. Just as it is important to accustom oneself to a particular type of paper, so one should familiarize oneself with a particular implement.

Washed drawing; draft sketch in pencil. The example shown is painted with water-colours, using strongly diluted pigments. The more darkly toned areas were achieved by applying several layers or washes of paint. The striking paleness of colour is partly the result of dilution, but is also caused by the presence of impurities in the form of other residual pigments; (cf. Colour Character, p. 98).

Single-Tone Painting – Washed Drawings

The first and simplest step in mastering water-colour technique is perhaps the application of a single colour tone. This technique, known as washing, consists of applying a coat of coloured liquid (e.g. diluted Indian ink) to a finished drawing. This leads firstly to a darkening or toning down of larger areas of the drawing. Secondly, by applying further washes, shadow effects can be achieved. Should certain sections of the drawing be obscured in the process, they can be drawn in again subsequently. In order to avoid waviness in the paper when wetted, a stouter quality of cartridge paper or water-colour paper should be used.

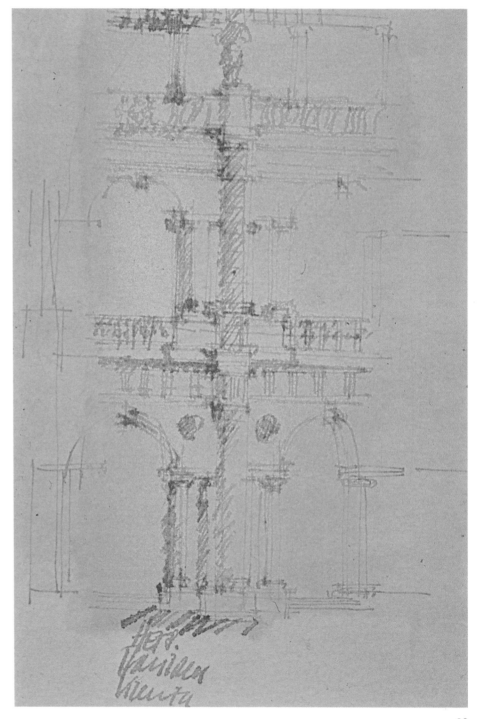

Washed drawing; draft sketch in sepia ink. Areas of shadow executed with brush and diluted ink. Details retouched with pen afterwards.

Mixing Colours

We are familiar with the problems attached to mixing colours from the section dealing with coloured pencil work. When using water-colours, one should try at first to mix the secondary colours orange, green and purple from the primary colours blue, red and yellow. By continuing to mix these colours with each other, one obtains brown and grey tones. In terms of technique one has to differentiate between painting on dry paper or paper that has previously been moistened. In the former case (sometimes known as glazing) the layer of colour has to be dry before a further layer can be applied. In the latter case (washing) the colours are allowed to flow into each other on the paper. In both cases the colours mix to create new colour tones. It is of fundamental importance in this respect that the different layers of colour should remain transparent. It is ultimately immaterial, however, whether one chooses to paint on dry or moistened paper.

It is of course possible to use water-colours in a thick, opaque manner (e.g. Emil Nolde); but we shall not discuss this technique here. Some schools of painting encourage pupils to use a great deal of liquid in their work, in order to gain experience in the flow and running of colours. As long as one is painting flowers, landscapes or cloud formations, this technique is adequate. But if one wishes to create a concrete depiction of surfaces and volumes, it will be necessary to use the glazing technique.

As well as mixing colours on the actual paper, it is possible to mix them on the palette. In the shallow pans of the paint box specially created for this purpose one can mix pigments taken directly from the cakes of water-colour paint and then transfer the newly created colour tone to the picture. A small dab should first be tested at the edge of the sheet. In this way one can also check whether the brush is too wet.

Both mixing techniques should be tried out as a preliminary exercise before one sets about the actual task of painting. With increasing practice, however, these technical aspects will recede further and further into the background and one will automatically come to use one or the other kind of colour mixing method. One of the basic principles of water-colour painting is that one proceeds from light to dark. It is possible to lighten darker areas, but the technique involved in this is something approaching that of gouache.

Colour tones mixed in the water-colour box (palette) are applied, using a glazing technique, over other areas of colour, producing further colour changes (dry paper).

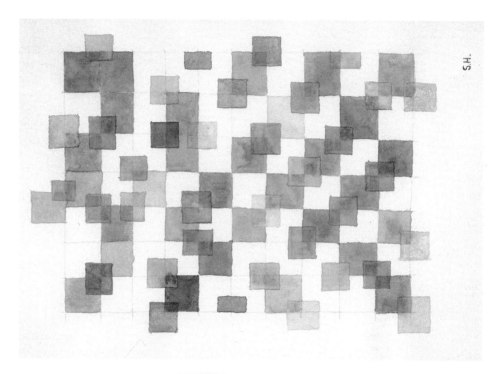

Colours applied to wetted paper flow into each other, creating new mixed tones. Coloured borders occur where the wetter areas dry out towards the surrounding dry surface of the paper.

Exercises in mixing technique: evenly applied layers of colour are superimposed on pre-drawn areas to create not merely mixed tones, but also an impression of spatial depth as a result of their transparency. The quality of luminosity is achieved by the use of pure colours.

An example of mixing colours in an imaginary landscape. The effect of spatial depth is achieved by keeping the colours in the background pale and by simplifying the forms.

Bad Weather in Agrigento. Application of a number of layers of paint on dry paper, using a technique akin to that of glazing. The green colour tone is modified in the area of the sky with light tints of blue and black. The striking effect of the edges between the areas of colour is the result of using low-absorbent paper.

Island in the Tiber, Rome. Initial application of colour to larger continuous areas wet on wet. After drying, the smaller forms were added in glazing technique, care being taken to achieve a balanced relationship between the colour tones.

Colour Relationships and Colour Character

We are already acquainted with the question of colour relationships from the examination of coloured pencil technique. Pure colours, as they exist in cake form, have a strongly luminous quality. In the process of mixing, the pigment is rendered »impure« to a certain extent, which gives rise to duller, somewhat greyish colour tones. It is important to be aware not merely of the distinction between light and dark, but of the contrast between bright and dull colours. Beginners tend to use pure tones, which leads to overcoloured pictures.

The choice of colours calls for a great deal of experience, but above all for a sense of harmony and disharmony. The effects achieved by using pure and toned down colours is something one can only learn by a process of experimentation. Useful in this respect are free exercises to test the effects of different quantities of paint and the intensity achieved. It is also worthwhile trying out the colour contrasts described in theoretical literature on the subject, although hardly any painter will follow these theories strictly in practice. Most instructive of all is the analysis of the coloration of existing paintings.

Comparison of pure and impure colour tones.

In Schönbuch. Pictorial composition, choice of colours and painting technique are all aimed at achieving a harmonious distribution of elements. Warm and cold, bright and subdued colour tones are set in relationship to each other.

The Coloured Drawing

The beginner should draw his subject before applying water-colours. The great advantage of this is that the various areas of the picture to be coloured are predefined by boundary lines. In addition, the preliminary drawing should help to determine the actual composition in advance. The sketch can then be coloured in, area for area. In the early stages the spatial perspective should be drawn as accurately as possible, whereby only the principal and secondary forms are necessary; (cf. pp. 20 ff., 33). The preliminary sketch should also be a simplified analytical representation. The details can be added with brush and paint. It is best to avoid hatching or shading in the drawing, so that the tonal surface values may be achieved purely by the application of colour.

With greater experience in painting, the preliminary drawing can be confined to a reproduction of the basic features of an object. In other words, one needs to draw only those things that are necessary for the pictorial elaboration in colour. This helps liberate the eye for the compositional qualities of the picture.

St. Mark's, Venice. The drawing itself forms a basic element of the depiction. It reveals the characteristic forms of the building and could exist in its own right without painted elaboration. The colours of the sky and the wall surfaces were applied on slightly moistened paper. The three-dimensional effect of the entrance portal is achieved by the repeated application of concentrated colour. The attraction of the picture as a whole lies in the range of abstraction it reveals – from the mere suggestion of forms to the concrete articulation of details.

The illustration still exhibits the character of a coloured drawing. The draft sketch
functions as a structural framework. Nevertheless, the depiction does manage to
liberate itself from its naturalistic model, in favour of a freer compositional treatment.

Ruins of Hadrian's Villa, Tivoli. The elements created by linear brush strokes have a similar function to a preliminary sketch and define the compositional framework. Insistence on a strictly representational character is gradually relinquished.

Reduction of Preliminary Drawing

Having progressed to a more advanced stage, one will be increasingly able to forgo the help of a preliminary drawing. The application of colour will no longer follow the pre-drawn lines. A prerequisite for this, however, is the ability to visualize the appearance of the finished picture in advance. If this is not successful, one can subsequently draw in details and lend a certain order to the poorer, unclear parts of the depiction and make it more cohesive or concrete. The drawn sections of a picture can also be articulated as a compositional complement to the planar, painted areas. Pen or pencil lines can be replaced relatively simply and effectively by brush strokes, where sharply delineated outlines are required. Even shading or hatching effects can be achieved in this way with the brush.

The decisive factor is that a restrained drawing allows greater liberty for pictorial fantasy; indeed, it stimulates it.

San Gimignano. Water-colour sketch without any preliminary drawing. The depiction is composed purely of areas of colour.

Palatine Hill, Rome. The preliminary drawing disappears behind the composition of coloured surfaces.

Pisa – Campo Santo. Here the preliminary drawing does no more than suggest the underlying rhythmic framework of the building. Linear depiction is by means of brush strokes.

Towers of the Basilica of Melk. The ornamentation typical of this building is reproduced in shorthand-like brush strokes. The picture thus acquires a thematic content.

Interpretation Through Pictorial Thinking

Over and above representational forms of depiction, drawing and painting provide scope to interpret the things we see in a more subjective manner. In the realm of architecture this may take the form of symmetries, geometric orders, or rhythmic sequences. Light and shade, plasticity and coloration can also provide the thematic motifs of a picture. In the final analysis it is the significance of the object in its own context that stimulates the artist to study it in painted form.

Leaving aside all representational considerations, therefore, it is the formal (Gestalt) qualities of the object that may become the pictorial statement, freely interpreted in terms of directional elements, stratification and superimposition. Alternatively, the artist's will to create forms in a free manner may find inspiration in architecture and move in realms that are no longer decipherable to the observer.

Santa Maria Formosa in Venice. Interplay of light and shadow during the evening.

Urban Landscape, Rome. The subject of the picture is the addition and overlapping effect of built forms, in which a rhythm is created by the towers and domes. (Additional use of soluble crayon.)

Island in the Tiber, Rome. Group of buildings with tall towers, like a ship in the waters
of the Tiber; (accentuation by means of pen strokes with sepia ink).

110

Palace in Ellwangen. Architecture and landscape as a composition of colours and forms. Increasingly free painting technique using white glazes that help to create milky mixed tonal values. Darker layers of colour can be painted over or brightened by using this technique, which in fact moves away from pure water-colour painting towards a concept more closely related to the glazing techniques used in oil painting.

Index of Drawings